DEAR MR. PRESIDENT

GREAT QUOTATIONS PUBLISHING COMPANY
GLENDALE HEIGHTS, ILLINOIS

Edited by: Rod Guge
Cover Illustration by Darrin Thompson
Typesetting and Page Design by: Bostrom Publishing, Inc.

Published in Glendale Heights, Illinois by Great Quotations Inc.

Printed in Hong Kong

INTRODUCTION

Every four years it happens. We, the people of America, entrust our livelihoods and our hopes to some guy who looks good in a suit. And then we give him four years to make things better.

We should pat ourselves on the back because we do our part. We get out, we vote, and we go home to see who won. And then we stay home for the most part, for the next four years, watching TV news reports and waiting to see if our new Executive Officer will remember that we put him there. To see if he'll remember all the things he said he'd do, all the ways he said he would help.

Most importantly, we wait to see if he'll remember all the things we said while he was canvassing the country soliciting our votes. Before an election, the lines of communication always seem very open. But once we've cast our vote, played our trump card and and the election is over, suddenly nobody seems to be asking a lot about what we want anymore. For that, we usually have to wait until the next election.

But we Americans are an impatient lot and we'd rather not wait four years to tell the President what's going on in our collective minds. We'd rather just go ahead and remind him now about some things that are important, about some things we'd like for him to hear.

That's what this book is about. Americans of all ages and backrounds were invited to tell what they'd like to say to the President. The result is an open letter from the people of America to their President. Some of the things we have to say are serious, which is good: We're in a serious situation in this country. Some of the things are funny, which is good, too: Given the state we're in, we need to keep a sense of humor.

This book could well mark the first time that Americans of all ages and states have come together to compile a collection of thoughts to send the President.

Who knows? Maybe in some small way, this book could make a difference. That's assuming, of course, that the President cares enough to read it. Meanwhile, God bless us all.

And God bless America

The responses presented in Dear Mr. President have been contributed by people of all ages, all backgrounds and all 50 states. Since America is a melting pot of opinions and thoughts, the goal of this ongoing project is to produce a book series that presents a rainbow of thoughts -- thoughts that make you laugh, some that prompt a tear, some that challenge your way of thinking, and maybe a few that inspire you to throw the book across the room.

When we take time to understand each other, then we're each doing our part to make America a better place. If this book series can help achieve that -- even to a small degree -- that it has been worth all the time and effort it took to develop.

Thanks so much to all the folks on these pages who took the time and effort to share how they feel.

Josh Max, Dorothy Elliott, A.C. Ramsey, Alan Sparrow, Brandon Castor, Paige Leitman, B. Wittelsberger, Steve Goodman, Dawn Matschke, Tiffany Graetz, Dee Southwood Blakey, Cynthia Felty, Ed Castor, John Paul Spiridakis, David A. Elizondo, Dennis McGrath, M. Setlock, David Simons, Uncle Junky, Barbara Miedema, Becki Fogle, Kent Alexander, Jack D'Alelio, An Bartel, Amy Fong, Jenny Palmer, Zac Willette, Amy Rutkowski, Brooke Craig, Karen Butenko, Caren Lissner, Megan Lissner, Steven Trujillo, Karen Dorsett, Andrea Defusco, Laura Stride, Carmen Kunze, Lawrence J. Pippick, L. Houle Gutierrez, Carole Vance, Phaedra Sharpe, Wayne Barnes, Marissa Maciel, Michael Blau, Patrick Robbins, T. Wolf Bolz, Kristyn Shaffer, Stephen Meyer, Dawn K. Gupta,Tallie Conner, David Ziegenhagen, Perrin Patterson, L.L. Baldwin, Randall Cook, Barbara Affrunti, Josh Modell, Roy Henock, Harlen Walsh, Nancy Peters, Connie Auer, Grace Andrus, Sandra Lynn Sabo, Robert Phillip O'dell, Kevin Miller, Mary Bieber, Linda O'Connell, Ginger Sharp Brown, Terry Brown, Kayci Rothweiler, Connie Johnson, Walt Wentz, Jim Knauff, Ginny Knauff, Jeremy Knauff, James Knauff, Jordan Knauff, Ward S. Krause, Louise Sullivan, Bob Brunner, Nancy C. Barnes,Sharon Boone, Robin Conover, Cathleen Cope, Diane Gahner, Wanda Conley, Teresa Garland, Kimberly Long, Heather Berry, John Kirby, Greg Kingdon, Forrest Bradley, Ken Astrup, Susan Pegden, Bill Perry, Lynn Bartlett, James V. Chambers, Teres Lambert, Terri R. Taylor-Hamrick, Karl W. Hockmeyer, Myrna Dossert, Myron Casey, Lee Chamblee, Beth Byron, Kathy Hayes, Suzanne Gordon, Gordon Gee, Lesa Taylor, Maryann Fosby, Neil Christiansen, Ashley Guge, Tyler Guge, Julie Murfitt, Kathy Penry, Pam Brunet, Anna Harbourt, Ann Geiszler, T.C. Whitehurst, Meredith Libbey, Randolph Melick, Linda Cochran, Tom Harmon, Ramona Mackenroth, Pam Karg, Jean Reid, Patrick Sharp, William Miller, Charles Baker, Raymond Smith, Leigh Ann Pettus, Jeff Pettus, Clara Bass, Ted Teague, Linda Slater, Anna Harbourt, Dale Loudermilk, James DiFonzo, Janet B. Gardner, Kay Stirling, BeLinda Sizemore, Mary Jane Niemann, Mary H. Jackson, Lydia Tompkins, Denise Onstad, Melissa Ann Boyer, Mary K. Hartle, Desiree Moore, Mildred Llucille Dressel, Lester Mitchell, Thelma Allen.

Mr. President Clinton

**Please would you lower taxes for Petes sake.
Thank you!**

*-John David Sisemore II
Age 7, Oklahoma*

I'd like to say to the President:

Instead of letting people sit around on welfare with nothing to do and no jobs to find, give them something to do for the money they're receiving from the government. How about a 9-to-5 Community Clean-Up Program? Anything they could do to earn their pay would make them feel more like useful citizens and less like societal cast-offs. And it might help get a few neighborhoods cleaned up.

And I'd like to say:

I'm not really for animal testing. But if you do intend to keep letting scientists conduct horrendous laboratory tests on animals, give me a call. There's a real obnoxious dog across the street that deserves a chance to serve society.

-Research assistant (F), Age 37, Nebraska

I'd like to say to the President:

Are you sorry you took the job yet?

-Singer/songwriter/musician/writer/painter (M),
Age 31, New York

I'd like to say to the President:

All things considered, Bill, I think it's time you started inhaling.

-Photographer (M), Age 39,
North Carolina (via New York via California)

I'd like to say to the President:

Why do you suppose abortion or choice is even a government issue at all?

I'd like to say to the President:

How long do you think it will be before we see a minority as President?

-Communications coordinator (F),
Age 27, New York

I'd like to say to the President:

Don't pander to nations that suppress human rights. We're a country that stands for freedom. Not just within our own boundries, but throughout the world.

And I'd like to say:

I need a job.

*-Educational psychologist Ph.D. candidate
(back in school again because I couldn't find a job with
just two Bachelor degrees and a Master's) (F),
Age 33, North Carolina*

14

I'd like to say to the President:

At this writing, it's less than a year since your election and you've already gone back on several of your campaign promises, but that's O.K. You can still redeem yourself. . .

. . . There are certain things that no human being can live without. These are air, water and food. If your Presidency can make sure that U.S. citizens do all that they can to clean up our air and water, and to ensure that food supplies will be clean and wholesome for future generations, then I'll vote for you again.

-Marine biologist (F), Age 22, Georgia

I'd like to say to the President:

Who is authorizing some of these weird studies being done for millions of dollars that seem so ridiculous? Who needs to conduct experiments to determine the salt content of gorilla perspiration when we don't need any experiments to know that people are starving and homeless in America?

And I'd like to say:

Let's get more government spending under control! If you'd spend more time on creating peace, we could trim billions from the military budget.

-Dental assistant (F), Age 45, North Dakota

I'd like to say to the President:

Do you admire John Kennedy more for being a great politician, or more for the ability he had to keep his own extramarital affairs out of the newspapers?

-Homemaker (F), Age 43, Oklahoma

I'd like to say to the President:

Love the one you're with.

-Student (F), Age 19, Georgia

I'd like to say to the President:

--Listen, Bill, I don't care who you sleep with -- just LEAD! Move it, man -- we gotta get at some of these problems. If you've got the guts, we've got the time and the will.

-Corporate director of government affairs (M),
Age 47, Ohio

I'd like to say to the President:

Why don't you kick congress in the butt?

-Insurance broker (M), Age 26, Utah

Dear Mr. President:

If I were in your shoes, here's what I'd do:
I'd steal a page out of Dave Barry's book and
establish the Department of Marge. Marge
would be a woman, mid-30's, with a couple
of kids and a mortgage, earning 20 grand a year.
All federal expenditures would require her
approval to become law . . .

. . . So the military brass, for example, would ask, "Marge, can we have a couple of skillion dollars for some neat-o, high-tech, computer-activated, blue-chip toilet paper covers (or whatever), and Marge would say, "No."

Would tend to eliminate government waste and mismanagement of funds, huh?

-Communications engineer (M), Age 42, Florida

I'd like to say to the President:

Speeding tickets should be waived for mothers carpooling small children with weak bladders.

And I'd like to say. . .

When foreign investors come over for visits, it's important for us to put on the best face we can. That's why former fashion models should be treated just like former military personnel and receive a stipend and insurance for the rest of their lives, in addition to a number of cosmetics subsidies.

-Legal clerk and former fashion model (F),
Age 33, Hawaii

I'd like to say to the President:

Don't let interest rates go back up until after I've had a chance to buy a new car.

-Graphic artist (M), Age 37, Texas

I'd like to say to the President:

Would you mind having a little talk with my boss?
He's starting to get on my nerves, if you know
what I mean.

-and-

Let's trade jobs for awhile and you'll see what
real pressure is.

-Accountant (F), Age 51, Virginia

Dear Mr. President:

Which do you think is worse: People who
are gay, because they were born that way,
or people who are left-handed, because they
were born that way? Neither of them asked
to be the way they are, and neither of them
has any power to change it. . .

. . .There was a time in this country when women were denied the right to pursue equality in terms of housing or jobs, when Blacks were denied the right to eat in certain restaurants or shop in certain stores. Those are milder versions of the kinds of rights that are being denied now to people who are gay. When will the Presidency stop bowing to the opinion of bigots, Americans, not just those who fit a certain mold.

-Computer technician (F), Age 42, Colorado

I'd like to say to the President:

How much did you weigh before you started jogging?

And I'd like to say:

Since the Bible condemns homosexuality, why do you condone it?

- and -

Guess who I voted for.

-Deputy clerk, caterer & die-hard Republican (F),
Age 50, Tennessee

I'd like to say to the President:

Would you mind playing the sax for my company's annual picnic?

- Administrative assistant (F), Age 50, Wyoming

I'd like to say to the President:

Every minute you spend playing the saxaphone
is one less minute you have to think about
solving our economic problems.

-Elementary teacher (F), Age 49, Alabama

I'd like to say to the President:

You've already demonstrated flip-flops on your promises about Haiti, public schooling, a reduction in the White House staff and the Congressional staff, the budget deficit reduction, gays in the military and so on and so forth.

It's time to start keeping your promises -- and to stop making indulgent ones that you can't or won't keep.

-University professor (M), Age 51, New Hampshire

I'd like to say to the President:

I know you're catching a lot of flack for the stand you've tried to take on certain things, but God bless you for at least trying to upset the status quo. For the first time in years, I feel like someone in the White House gives a damn about me.

-Department store manager (M), Age 35, Ohio

I'd like to say to the President:

Now that you've tackled a few of the major issues, it's time to do some thinking about what kind of necklace Hillary will make famous (pearls went out with Barbara Bush).

-Student (F), Age 19, Georgia

Here's what I wish I could say to the President:

Thank you for balancing the budget, creating
world peace, cutting taxes and making this
country a wonderful place in which to live.
Now we're all wondering what you're going
to do during the next two years of
your administration.

-Executive secretary (F), Age 28, New York

Dear Mr. President:

Here's something to try the next time you're daydreaming: Pretend like you've just seen your doctor, and he told you that you have just four years to earn your place in history while winning the gratitude of the American people and of people throughout the world. . .

...At the end of those four years, the world will either end in deprivation and/or total thermonuclear destruction, OR it can be a peaceful, prosperous place to live and work, all depending on how you conduct yourself during the four-year period.

Then wake up and realize it's not pretend at all.

-Hospital public relations director (F), Age 36, Iowa

I'd like to say to the President:

**Remember that war kills people.
I'm a great grandmother, and I've
seen too many people die.**

-Retired schoolteacher (F), Age 78, Wyoming

I'd like to say to the President:

Never talk about hating broccoli. Broccoli farmers vote, too. Just ask George Bush.

- and -

Here's a good rule of thumb: Never say "Read my lips" to the media.
Learn from your predecessors.

-Lobbyist (M), Age 44, Tennessee

I'd like to say to the President:

Do whatever you have to do. Just please, work with the Congress to move our country forward and to reduce our serious debt. I'm sick to death of hearing each President say, "It's all their fault," and then hearing Congress say, "It's all his fault." Sometimes I think it's all our fault for electing a bunch of finger-pointers in the first place.

-Professor (M), Age 58, Indiana

Please come up with a plan to re-work the Social Security system so our young people won't feel it will be extinct when they get old. And visit the homeless and the poor so you can get a better picture of their struggles and their sense of hopelessness. If you have to, phase out the space program while people here are going hungry.

-Secretary (F), Age 58, Oregon

I'd like to say to the President:

Use public opinion polls in your decision-making process. That way, you could actually go back to a government of the people, by the people and for the people.

-Retired firefighter (M), Age 59, Alabama

I'd like to say to the President:

Remember when your family might have had trouble paying the bills? Help us out, bud!

-Assistant editor (F), Age 29, Missouri

I'd like to say to the President:

If Hollywood were going to make a movie about your life, who would you want to play yourself? Who would play Hillary? How about Chelsea? What about Socks?

And I'd like to say:

Would you and Mrs. Clinton ever consider having more children? Would you feel comfortable bringing more children into the world, given the future you envision for America 20 or 25 years down the road?

-Student (F), Age 17, Arkansas

I'd like to say to the President:

Education should be the top of your priorities.
Not just formal education within the school
systems, but social education, as well: If this
country is to survive as a free society, Americans
must learn not to hate one another just because
some of us are different than others. And health
education: We all must learn to take better care
of ourselves physically and emotionally.
Education on all levels is the only way for us
to do this and meet the challenges and
opportunities the future will have to offer.

And I'd like to say:

Don't abuse your power. Remember where you came from and remember who you work for.

We put you in the White House, and we can just as easily kick you out.

-Healthcare administrator (M), Age 29, Washington

I'd like to say to the President:

Hard decisions are seldom popular, but they're frequently necessary.

- and -

When things get rough, remember you wanted this job.

-Executive assistant, Office of the Governor (F),
Age 42, Alaska

51

I'd like to say to the President:

Never create an adversarial atmosphere with other countries just so you'll look like a tough guy here in the state -- even when election time rolls around. I'd rather see my husband at home, and alive, than to see you playing Billy the Kid.

-Service agency manager (F), Age 32, Tennessee

I'd like to say to the President:

If your views are so different from those of Congress, why do you dress so much like them?

-Industrial salesperson (M), Age 50, California

One day I'd like to say to the President:

You have a run in your pantyhose, ma'am.

-Attorney (F), Age 29, Michigan

I'd like to say to the President:

Since you are probably one of the least qualified Presidents ever to take office, please don't let your ineptness cause you to put further restrictions on an already overburdened economy. The only way this economy will surivive is to let it breathe, and those breaths have to be big, deep ones!'

-Economist (M), Age, California

I'd like to say to the President:

Don't let the bastards get you down.

-Air traffic controller (M), Age 38, New York

I'd like to say to the President:

If we can send men to the moon, why can't we make a pair of pantyhose that lasts a week?

-Court stenographer (F), Age 25, Delaware

I'd like to say to the President:

When you're in a public place, do Secret Service men go into the bathroom with you? What if it's just a single-stall bathroom?

I'd like to say to the President:

Don't try to set moral standards by laws restricting actions of individuals but by programs that lead by example. Remember, you can't legislate morality.

And I'd like to say:

Listen to the people -- not the PAC's.
Political action committees might have helped
fund your campaign, but that doesn't give
them the right to run the nation.

-Photojournalist (F), Age 25, Arizona

I'd like to ask the President:

When you're in the White House alone, and you light a fire in the fireplace and it starts to smoke, do you inhale?

And I'd like to ask:

Do you ever send flowers to your wife? If so, do you pay for them out of your own pocket, or do taxpayers pick up the bill because you have a White House florist do it?

-Architect (M), Age 26, Louisana

I'd like to say to the President:

**You should make the daily eating of chocolate
a federal mandate.**

-Governor's staff (M), Age 37, Rhode Island

I'd like to say to the President:

Why does a fishing license have to be renewed every year when a gun permit doesn't?

-Country music singer (M), Age 32, Tennessee

I'd like to say to the President:

Just a reminder, Bill: You didn't get close to a majority of votes, and Hillary didn't get any.

-Copy store manager (M), Age 37, Idaho

I'd like to say to the President:

Our very first First Lady was a career woman who made more money than her husband and whose support was vital in allowing George to fight in the Revolution and later run for President. Do you think people will ever realize that it takes an intelligent, strong, secure man to have a relationship with an intelligent, strong woman?

-Physician (F), Age 43, Wyoming

I'd like to say to the President:

For a radical approach, maybe you can appoint Jack Kemp as a "Cities Czar." Lord knows our urban areas need fixing, and the man seems to claim he knows how to do it.

If it works, you'll justly get most of the credit for improvement. If it doesn't, the man won't be a very credible opponent, nor will any who identified with him.

-Civil engineer (M), Age 46, Connecticut

I'd like to say to the President:

Remember what happened to Julius Caesar? Watch out for your buddies and advisors, Bill.

-Musician (F), Age 31, Vermont

Dear Mr. President:

Being a child of the '60s and a woman, I've always considered myself uniquely qualified to dispense Presidential advice. Furthermore, I've often wondered why the government hires all these high-priced people for advisory positions when they can get someone with a higher I.Q. and more common sense for half the price, someone who even drives her own car.
I have lots of good ideas. . .

. . .For example, I would have told you in a heartbeat not to get that haircut. I also think that we should designate a portion of each individual's income tax, say 30 percent, to be used for whatever that taxpayer chooses -- more jobs, better schools, road repair, more law enforcement, guns for Iran, whatever. The other 70 percent would be used as it always has been -- for government waste, limos and inflated government employee paychecks. If Americans had this kind of opportunity, not only would they be less hostile when tax time rolls around, but they might even kick in a few extra bucks, if you ask me.

-Registered nurse in labor & delivery (F), Age 39, Florida

I'd like to say to the President:

Remember Pericles:
"Where there is no vision the people perish."
It is better to be scorned as a tax-and-spend
visionary than praised as a
borrow-and-mortgage skinflint.

-High school teacher and counselor (M), Age 40, California

I'd like to say to the President:

Attempting to "please all of the people all of the time" tends to alienate all of the people by election time.

Happy retirement.

-U.S. Postal Service letter carrier (M), Age 38, California

I'd like to say to the President:

Stick to your guns on fighting homophobia in the military. Don't let them discharge people simply because of their orientation.

And I'd like to say:

Leapfrog the "managed care" option and push for a single payer health care system that assures quality health care for everyone. Sure, it will be somewhat more expensive. But the actual cost per citizen will be miniscule -- pennies per year -- and all the taxpayers I know would be glad to pay that for the comfort of knowing their health concerns will be taken care of.

-Health care executive (M), Age 56, Minnesota

I'd like to say to the President:

All parents in the nation think those people who make malicious remarks about your child are jerks. And most of us think you shouldn't wear shorts when you jog around television cameras.

-Syndicated newspaper humor columnist (M),
Age 40, Arizona

I'd like to say to the President:

Please don't embarrass me. In the days following your election, I went around to all my Republican friends shrieking, "Neener, neener, neener," and doing that obnoxious fist of victory thing. If you screw up, it will reflect very badly on me. I have tolerated the GOP's "holier-than-thou" attitude for waaaaay too long.

Make me proud.

Make them grovel.

-Owner/operator of a plant (the green kind)
maintenance service (F), Age 44, California

I'd like to say to the President:

**Bill, you don't call, you don't write.
What gives???**

-Manager (F), Age 47, Virginia

I'd like to say to the President:

**Good morning, Mr. President.
Thanks for the appointment.**

-Co-op director (M), Age 41, North Dakota

This is what I wish I could say to the President:

Thanks for the offer, but I already have a job.
- or better yet -
Good night, honey.

-Contracts negotiator (F), Age 32, Connecticut

Here's what I'd like to say to the President:

**Here's your speech, sir.
Edit to your heart's content.**

-Speechwriter (F), Age 28, Rhode Island

This is what I wish I could say to the President:

Gee, Dad, I can't see the Washington Monument from that bedroom. Is it okay if I have one over on the other wing?

-Student (F), Age 13, Maine

Here's what I'd like to say:

**Keep your cat indoors. Socks will live a longer,
healthier life that way.**

-Technical writer (F), Age 42, New Jersey

I'd like to say to the President:

Do well on the crime issue and you won't have to have done perfectly on the economy to be re-elected.

-Printing plant worker (M), Age 34, Illinois

If I had the opportunity to speak to Bill Clinton. . .

I'd appologize that I didn't vote for him and I would thank him for trying so hard to make things happen for this country in the short time he has been our President. I would let him know that I pray for him and his health and well-being every day.

-Marketing administrator for a software development division of a Fortune 500 computer conglomerate; also, single mother of a 6-1/2-year-old daughter; college graduate; Christian (F), Age ??, California

I'd like to say to the President:

I understand that you are as human as I am, and therefore will make mistakes. When weighing decisions, think about every person you will affect, and use your discretion. You can't please everyone, so be ready for criticism from those who do not like what you decide.

-College student (Spanish major, F), Age 22, Michigan

Here's what I'd like to say to the President:

**Hey Bill, could you loan me a twenty 'til payday?
(I mean, what better way to assure
that I'd get a job?)**

*-Aspiring writer (i.e., "unemployed, ") (M),
Age 22, Maine*

Here's some things I'd like to say to the President:

- Ever think about giving Gore a charisma transplant?

- Is it true that when Stephen King wrote *Sleepwalkers*, he really was writing about members of Reagan's Cabinet?

- Do you ever ask for grits in the White House?

- What are your plans once you're out of office in '96?

- The bit about not inhaling was hysterical. Did you ever do stand-up?

- The category: Presidential Involvements; the Jeopardy answer: "Flowers, marijauna and Vietnam."

-Producer (M), Age ??, California

I'd like to say to the President:

When things like cable TV rates and airline fares are regulated by the government, why the hell aren't things as basic and as important as medical rates regulated as well? Why aren't many doctors, many of whom are making a half-million a year (or more), simply given a ceiling on the price they can charge for treatments? It's ridiculous. . .

. . .In many states, telephone service rates are regulated because telephones are considered a basic necessity. Is health care any less a basic necessity? In my opinion, any country that makes its elderly and sick sell their homes and lose lifetime savings to receive something as basic as medical treatment is a country that verges on barbarism. Please stop letting the American Medical Association and the Insurance Association twist your arm, and maintain your stand on quality medical treatment for every American. I'm going to send this same request to my Congressmen.

-Free-lance writer (M), Age 35, Kansas

I'd like to say to the President:

Vietnam was an example of the mis-use of the military by the executive. If you decide to do anything militarily in Yugoslavia, be prepared for innocent civilians to die. If you're not prepared for that, keep the military out. Don't send them in to be targets and tie their hands because you are afraid civilians will be killed if they do the job right.

Remember: Desert Storm worked because the executive turned the military loose and allowed them to do their job.

-History teacher (M), Age 37, West Virginia

I'd like to say to the President:

The United States should not, on its own initiative, be the police force or the moral conscience for the world. We should cooperate with U.N. initiated activities, but we should not take the lead as we did in Desert Storm and as we are in Africa and the Balkans.

-Healthcare executive (M), Age 56, Minnesota

I'd like to say to the President:

We told you the deficit was that bad. You didn't believe it. Or did you really not know?

I don't have your brains or education, but I knew.

-Homemaker (F), Age 51, Idaho

I'd like to say to the President:

Have you ever wondered how it feels to be a female living in a country where you can't take a walk through your neighborhood without fear of being mugged or raped or killed?. . .

And I'd like to say:

If you suddenly became a woman, how do you think it would feel to have your salary cut by 20 percent just because you don't need a zipper in the front of your trousers?

And one more thing:

If the Equal Rights Amendment were passed, discrimination against women probably wouldn't end. But we would, at least, be living in a country that has enough of a conscience to say, "This is wrong."

-High school teacher (F), Age 44, Mississippi

I'd like to say to the President:

I'm a divorced mother of two teenage boys. I make $26,000 a year in a job that should pay more. My ex-husband's record with child-support is spotty at best, and it's not likely to change when they enter college. I know, as my sons do, that their best hope for a better life is to work hard and do well in school. . .

. . .It's not going to be easy. Three people living on my salary can barely get by, even without college expenses. Yet the federal government has the gall to tell me I make too much money for us to qualify for financial aid. Here's what I have to say: Try it yourself, then tell me again how I make too much to deserve college aid for my children.

-Office manager (F), Age 36, Nevada

I'd like to say to the President:

When it comes to issuing "temporary" tax hikes and the like, I hope you'll remember this: There is nothing more permanent than something the government does temporarily.

-High school teacher (M), Age 37, Indiana

I'd like to say to the President:

Please, please do not make my life a living hell
to live. I am convinced that within two years,
I will be paying more taxes than I am now
because of your plans, despite the assurances
you've given me. I can't afford anymore.

-Software engineer (M), Age 25, California

I'd like to say to the President:

Watch out for any vans parked across the street
with one-way glass windows.

-Production manager (M), Age 43, Connecticut

I'd like to say to the President:

Next time, try jogging into a Burger King.

-Fast food manager (guess which chain),
(M), Age 37, New Mexico

Dear Mr. President:

I think you should get a dog and name him Shoes.

-Pet store manager (F), Age 27, Hawaii

Dear Mr. President:

When I think of you, I think of a white horse, not the White House.

-Banker (F), Age 32, Tennessee

Dear Mr. President:

We should abolish the practice of paying welfare recipients extra money for each child they have; instead, let's establish free day-care services on existing school grounds and provide the children with two meals a day. . .

...That way, we'll be sure they're being fed with the money that is intended to provide them with necessities. And, we won't be paying parents to have children they might not even want just to get additional money from the government. This would allow single parents who are on welfare to get out and work, since they wouldn't be forced to stay home and watch their children during the day.

-Writer (M), Age 31, North Carolina

I'd like to say to the President:

Don't get bogged down in any sort of Vietnam, either foreign or domestic. And never assume that high popularity means you're politically safe unless you answer the needs of the American people.

-Journalist (F), Age 62, Montana

I'd like to say to the President:

Now that you've been in office for awhile, I hope
you'll can the "new generation" stuff.
You're not Jack Kennedy, and Americans did
not vote for Jack Kennedy in 1992. Although
many of your juniors voted for you, many
of your seniors did, too. We're not young
anymore, but we still deserve the same objective
considerations that the baby boomers already
receive. You're now President of us all.

-Retired engineer (M), Age 77, Utah

I'd like to say to the President:

Keep on doing what you're doing. The world would be a much better place without people like Reagan, Bush and especially Bob Dole.

-Retiree (M), Age 85, North Carolina

I'd like to say to the President:

Each child deserves the best education he or she can absorb. And they each need to learn about more than just math and biology. Given the world of problems children now have to face, a complete education should include required courses on self-development, self-esteem, basic household care and the devastating effects of drug and violence on individuals and on society as a whole.

-Elementary school principal (F), Age 42, California

Dear Mr. President:

Here's my best advice: Simply leave the economy alone, let it cure itself, sit back and take credit for it, and you will be a shoe-in for re-election in '96.

-Botanist (F), Age 28, Pennsylvania

Dear. Mr. President:

I think you -- and every other President --
would do a better job, and our country would
be better off, if the Executive Officers really
would focus all their time and energy on the
four years they've been given rather than
thinking so much about the next term
A lot of us hope you'll try that.

-Petroleum engineer (M), Age 49, Texas

I'd like to say to the President:

I voted for you this time, Bill, but it's because I'm counting on you not to screw things up any more than they are.

-Hotel director and father of three (M), Age 45, Georgia

Dear Mr. President:

Open up a small portion of the Arctic National
Wildlife Refuge to oil and gas development.
It would help not only my state,
but the economy as a whole.

- and -

If you ever need a top-notch secretary,
give me a call.

-Executive secretary (F), Age 36, Alaska

Dear Mr. President:

It's good to know that you and Vice President Gore have a commitment to helping the environment. But please remember that environmental policies must also take into consideration the impacts they will have on people and business.

-Public relations executive (F), Age 34, Florida

Dear Mr. President:

Think about all of our tomorrows -- not just yours. Preach, live and encourage the people of this nation to be diverse without being divisive.

-Corporate administrator (M), Age 37, Iowa

I'd like to say to the President:

You're surrounded by sycophants. Listen to your critics instead of condemning them.

-Advertising executive (F), Age 31, New York

I'd like to say to the President:

I'd feel better if you'd watch at least one movie a week about the way the middle class lives. It's going to be awfully easy for you to forget all that when you're being tooled around in bullet-proof limousines all the time.

-News reporter (M), Age 31, South Dakota

I'd like to say to the President:

Put more women in your political positions. But make sure they know how to keep the law before you appoint them.

One more thing: Tell Geoge Bush that nobody cared about his dog.

-Ag journalist (F), Age 43, Colorado

I'd like to say to the President:

We have to investigate welfare and workers' compensation fraud because I see it even in my own small community. We must get rid of free government handouts. And, as a general rule, we need to clean house. It could do us all some good.

-Secretary to the Governor (F), Age 56, Montana

I'd like to say to the President:

**When are politicians going to wake up and
realize there is a value to maintaining
people in rural America?**

-Co-op director (M), Age 41, North Dakota

I'd like to say to the President:

**When's the last time you hung out in a laundromat? Or rode a public transportation bus? Or actually stood in line at Disney World?
Could do you -- and us -- some good.**

-College student (M), Age 22, Washington, D.C.

I'd like to say to the President:

Help to make, or re-make, this country into one nation under God.

-Homemaker and mother of three (F), Age 36, Georgia

I'd like to say to the President:

This country's not big enough for the two of us and a multi-trillion dollar deficit.

- and -

How many Presidents does it take to screw in a light bulb?

-Receptionist (F), Age 36, Arkansas

I'd like to say to the President:

Address the farm crisis and the economic crisis in rual America through a good rural development program. Rural America is still the bread basket of the world -- we produce some 70 percent of the world's food. If you let the rural economy suffer to a point at which farmers can't stay in business, you're asking for trouble. Not only for this country, but for the entire world.

And I'd like to say:

Reform the welfare system so single mothers can support their families through education and training. I did this myself through a War on Poverty program in the '60s. We need some programs like that now.

-Editor (F), Age 50, North Dakota

I'd like to say to the President:

I wish President Bush could have stuck around another four years. But since he couldn't, here's what I'd like you to hear: Don't give away our money when we are in such turmoil. Leave it at home instead of giving it to our neighbors.

-Administrative assistant (F), Age 46, Minnesota

I'd like to say to the President:

Get serious about population control worldwide.
Humans can't just go on breeding
indiscriminately forever.

- and -

Don't forget that you're a
public servant -- not a god.

-Corporate administrator (M), Age 37, Iowa

I'd like to say to the President:

- **If you want to make our school days longer, make your work days longer, too.**

- **How come the White House is white? How come the Oval Office is Oval?**

I'd like to say to the President:

• Did you ever visit a wax museum and see yourself?

• Tell the truth: Do you ever watch cartoons?

-Student (F), Age 10, Massachusetts

I'd like to say to the President:

**Set the example -- deeds speak louder
than words.**

-Dairyman (M), Age 60, Indiana

I'd like to say to the President:

"Hey buddy, keep your (double) chin up!"

-Full-time student/full-time record store slave (M),
Age 19, Wyoming

I'd like to say to the President:

Remember that, although special-interest lobbyists are citizens, they are not necessarily human.

-Education student (M), Age 19, Minnesota

I'd like to say to Bill Clinton:

How stupid do we look?

-Free-lance industrial education consultant;
Mom; part-time farmer and husband's best friend (F),
Age 36, New York

What would I say to Bill Clinton?

I'd ask him all the CIA/government secrets he must know by now--whether the government created HIV for population control, whether his own election victory was predetermined, whether UFO's are really abducting people in New Mexico, the whole bag. If he wouldn't tell me, I'd get Prime Time Live to do a big expose on McDonald's so he'd feel odd about his next box of McNuggets.

-Student (M), Age 22, Kansas

What would I like to say to Bill Clinton?

"**M**r. President, hair Number 192 is out of place. Here's a comb. Better take care of that."

-Cocktail waitress (F), Age 23, California

I'd like to say to the President:

- **G**et America back into the world market. We're losing the battle with Germany and Japan.

- **D**on't support legislation or Supreme Court nominees who want to take away even more of a woman's freedom over her own body. No 60-year-old man in Washington should have the right to tell me what I can do with my own body.

-Student, Math/German major (F), Age 20, Oklahoma

I'd like to say to the President:

You really went all the way to Martha's Vineyard for mango ice cream?

-English professor (F), Age 25, Massachusetts

I'd like to say to the President:

If you really want the American public to have faith in our public school system, you need to show some faith yourself. Put Chelsea back in a public school.

Also, if you re-decorated the Red Room, would you re-name it also? Just curious.

-College English major (F), Age 19, California

I'd like to say to the President:

Any chance we could outlaw the Arsenio Hall show, or maybe just sell it to some of our international enemies?

-Producer & free spirit (M), Age 46, California

I'd like to say to the President:

Dear Mr. Clinton,

I have the power to make birds levitate, but nobody seems to care. I just thought you should know.

-Student (M), Age 22, North Carolina

I'd like to say to the President:

If we were to have an affair, would it be alright if I called you Bill?

-Research librarian (F), Age 32, Maryland

Dear Mr. President:

I think you and your family are doing fine.
A few glitches out of the gate, maybe, but who's
counting? So many problems, so little time.
I only hope you will continue to listen to us -- to
the ordinary people who got such a charge out of
your becoming President. . .

. . .The concern you and Hillary show about health care, the advancement of women (and other minorities), and the general air of unpretentiousness you bring to the most important job in the U.S., promise a true new hope for us all. Please continue to add experienced people to your advisory circle, to balance the enthusiasm of the "kids" in the White House. Hang in there, keep jogging and take the critics with a grain of salt.

-Political advocate (F), Age ??, Colorado

I'd like to say to the President:

One way to save money is to cut spending within the hot lunch program at schools. I see tons of food thrown into the dumpster because the students either aren't hungry or would rather eat in a restaurant. There is money in their homes for cable TV, vacations, video rentals, bikes, the "hottest" sports shoes, clothes and toys. That indicates there's also money for food, if they want to eat it.

-2nd-grade teacher (F), Age 62, North Dakota

I'd like to say to the President:

When we live up to our responsibilities as citizens of America, we expect the same from our leaders. Within the independent sector, we have the power and resources to accomplish most of our medical and social needs. In too many cases, however, the government intervenes and botches things.
It's your choice: Do we get The American Dream, or will government ineptitude make it The American Nightmare?

-Writer (F), Age ??, Delaware

I'd like to say to the President:

I'm afraid my grandchildren's American dreams will get the ax with the continuing rise of the income tax. (I thought maybe if I made it rhyme you could remember it more easily).

-Senior citizen (F), Age 66, Oklahoma

I'd like to say to the President:

Think about moving the White House to Arkansas so people can swing by after visiting Branson, Missouri (we're the No. 1 tourist spot now!).

-Entertainer (M), Age 24, Missouri

I'd like to say to the President:

As I watch the moral decay and the flaunting of wickedness in our society, I'm reminded that no nation has long survived the violation of righteous principles. I hope you will not presume that we are somehow the exception. Please reject all counsel that advocates violation of spiritual principles, including violence, pornography and the homosexuals agenda. And remember that we all need to be wary of the subtle biases of the news media.

-Homemaker (F), Age ??, Florida

I'd like to say to the President:

Wouldn't it be nice if all the hate-mongering, pseudo-sanctimonious religious zealots in the world could take all that time and energy they spend on hating homosexuals and other races and direct it toward sheltering the homeless, or stopping child abuse, or feeding the hungry, or doing any of the millions of things that would indicate in some way that their religion is filled more with love than hatred? Any laws you could pass to that effect?

-Pharmacist and Christian who happens to be gay (M),
Age 42, South Carolina

I'd like to say to the President:

Please send help for this college kid who has just spent the past four years beating the books only to enter the real world to be beaten by the country's current economic crisis.

-Student (F), Age 19, Georgia

I'd like to say to the President:

And how does that make you feel. . .

-Psychologist (F), Age 34, Illinois

I'd like to say to the President:

**How did it feel to be elected
largely because, at the time, you seemed like
the lesser of several evils?**

-Graduate student (F), Age 23, New Mexico

I'd like to say to the President:

I was proud to cast my Democratic vote for you, and I think you hold a sincere dream in your heart for all Americans. You held a dream for an education, and you pursued it straight-forwardly. Despite obstacles along the way, you have proved you could make a difference in the lives of others. I wholeheartedly support you in your attempts to make a difference in so many lives now.

-Senior citizen (F), Age ??, Colorado

154

I'd like to say to the President:

After years of observing, I've come to the conclusion that a single four-year term apparently does not provide enough time for any President to sufficiently tax people to death. And that, apparently, is the reason for a second term. Give us a break and either get out after the first term or change the whole thought process about taxation during your Presidency, and we'll hope it lasts for years to come.

-Angry taxpayer (F), Age ??, Louisana

I'd like to say to the President:

Consider making a trip to the Holy Land.
It might help clear your focus on a lot
of confusing issues.

-Nursing home resident (F),
Age 85, South Dakota

I'd like to say to the President:

Just for the record, I serve residents of a large rural area, and there are times when I wish I had three clones. I was in college for the better part of a decade, and I worked my butt off then and now so that I can provide the best service possible to my patients. . .

. . .I often work 14-hour days, and I make way less than any United States Senator. So while you're thinking about the whole health-care issue, please remember that pharmaceutical companies, insurance companies and exorbitant malpractice suits are the biggest causes of escalating medical costs.

-Physician (M), Age 37, Oklahoma

I'd like to say to the President:

For unifying the 2-party system, have you considered divorcing Hillary and marrying Barbara Bush?

-Country music singer (M), Age 32, Tennessee

I'd like to say to the President:

Try Supercuts.

-Student (M), Age 20, New Hampshire

Dear Mr. President and Mrs. Clinton:

I feel you are a team, and I am proud to way you are my team. Both of you are setting an example for my daughters on teamwork in a marriage and a career. As for hopes and dreams you can help the country achieve, here goes my wish list. . .

. . .I would like mental health treatment, with a spending ceiling, to be part of our nation's healthcare plan. I would like all government and private offices to use recycled paper and other products. I would like a limit on immigration: How can we feed and welcome the world? I would like all children to have the opportunity to get free immunizations and a full stomach when they go to bed at night. . .

. . .I would like the government to be known as a thrifty organization, one that welcomes creative change. I would like my grandchildren to be able to experience some wilderness areas that are untouched by logging and the destruction that can come with progress.
I would love it if all young people served one year of public service to their country before they go on to higher education and marriage. . .

. . .I know these are lofty goals, but I can dream, can't I? Good luck to both of you. And remember that you can't please everyone. I tried for the first 40 years of my life, and it didn't work.

-Licensed professional counselor (F), Age ??, Colorado

Dear Mr. President:

I'm glad it's your job and not mine.

-Nanny (F), Age 32, Iowa

President Clinton, when you are making those decisions that will affect all our lives, we hope you will take the time to listen to the voices of America.

If you would like to participate in future volumes of
The America Says Book Series, please contact us at:.

The America Says Book Series
P.O. Box 40671
Nashville, TN 37204

FAX (615) 386-3959

OTHER TITLES BY GREAT QUOTATIONS PUBLISHING COMPANY